The Lighter Side of Teaching

Looking back on fun and games in and out of the classroom

The Lighter Side of Teaching

Looking back on fun and games in
and out of the classroom

Mereo Books

1A The Wool Market Dyer Street Cirencester Gloucestershire GL7 2PR
An imprint of Memoirs Publishing www.mereobooks.com

The Lighter Side of Teaching: 978-1-86151-901-6

First published in Great Britain in 2014
by Mereo Books, an imprint of Memoirs Publishing

Copyright ©2018

Scott Hamlyn has asserted his right under the Copyright Designs and Patents Act 1988 to be identified as the author of this work.

The author and publisher have made every effort to secure permission for all reproduced material. Any enquiries or concerns about copyright should be addressed to the publisher.

A CIP catalogue record for this book is available from the British Library. This book is sold subject to the condition that it shall not by way of trade or otherwise be lent, resold, hired out or otherwise circulated without the publisher's prior consent in any form of binding or cover, other than that in which it is published and without a similar condition, including this condition being imposed on the subsequent purchaser.

The address for Memoirs Publishing Group Limited can be found at www.memoirspublishing.com

The Memoirs Publishing Group Ltd Reg. No. 7834348

Typeset in 10/17pt Century Schoolbook
by Wiltshire Associates Publisher Services Ltd.
Printed and bound in Great Britain by Biddles Books

Contents

About the Author
Introduction
Acknowledgements

Chapter 1:	Training for what's to come	1
Chapter 2:	Into the real world	16
Chapter 3:	A year's supply teaching	25
Chapter 4:	Working in the independent sector	30
Chapter 5:	Reflection	83

About the Author

Scott Hamlyn taught geology and geography for over thirty years from the late 1970s, having gained a first degree in both subjects. This involved working in various types of secondary schools in the south, including secondary modern and comprehensive, finishing at a senior independent educational establishment. He also has a PGCE (Postgraduate Certificate in Education) and an MA in Earth Science Education, continuing that with PhD research.

Introduction

Teaching involves many assumed tasks such as lesson planning, marking, parents' evenings, staff meetings etc. For many years we have insisted on regular attendance, compliance, participation and obedience. Teachers give orders and expect certain standards of behaviour. Yet this would all seem, certainly to those outside education, to be somewhat less than amusing – more demanding, stressful and serious, even essential, career pre-requisites. Indeed, with a very prescriptive National Curriculum, GCSE and 'A' Level specifications detailing what should be taught and by when, time for humour would appear to be minimal. However, there are so many interactions every day between staff and pupils that humorous asides are inevitable, and they are usually welcome diversions.

Humour is one instructional tool that classroom teachers can use to increase their effectiveness. Theorists like Ziv (1979) suggest that humour stimulates curiosity, which is related to gaining and keeping pupils' attention, and that in turn is related to memory and learning outcomes, especially when the humour is linked to the subject matter. It also helps to establish a rapport with those pupils, along with reducing tension between the teacher and those taught, and this may well extend beyond the classroom into the school's extra-curricular activities.

A school inspector has said: "…humour is highly related to learning and adds inestimably to our life." (Phinn, 2004, p.58)

Of course, as we shall see, all this does not preclude comical asides and ad hoc humorous incidents involving the staff themselves.

Definition of 'funny':

1a. Causing laughter or amusement: a funny cartoon.
b. Making or given to making amusing jokes or witticisms: a colleague who is very funny.
2a. Difficult to account for; unusual or odd: "I had a funny feeling that she would call".
2b. Suspiciously odd: "It's funny how I seem to lose something every time he comes around".

(www.thefreedictionary)

A sense of humour? Simply put, you'll struggle in the classroom without one. An important aspect of an enthusiasm for teaching, as well as for life, is the ability to see and enjoy the funny things that surround us. While everyone likes a laugh, it's been shown that children laugh about ten times more than the average adult. Teachers, more than anyone, need to embrace this. Laughter makes every classroom a better place. It doesn't mean you have to act like Robin Williams every day; it just implies that you should never miss an opportunity to laugh with your pupils and at yourself.

Whilst every event in this book is based on real occurrences, as witnessed either by the author himself or directly by a close colleague and/or pupils, the identity of the individuals involved has been protected by the use of random letters for their real names. No responsibility is taken for any coincidental similarities which may occur. Similarly, teaching establishments have not been referred to by name or location.

Acknowledgements

I should like to thank all the colleagues and pupils who have contributed to this book and thereby, whether inadvertently or not, underpinned the whole tale.

I would also like to thank Giles/Express Newspapers/Express Syndication for their kind permission in allowing the use of Giles cartoons.

https://uk.pinterest.com/pin

Chapter 1

Training for what's to come

It all started with a University of Wales PGCE (Postgraduate Certificate in Education) course in the late 1970s. I thought I would give the course, and teaching, a try; I hardly felt a calling into the world's noblest profession at that stage.

The introductory part of the course was more of a continuation of the previous three years of first degree academia, cloistered in a ready-made built and social environment where almost everyone was of a similar age with broadly similar values and attitudes, reflecting but a very small pocket of the population in terms of age and social profile.

We had been adequately prepared as fledgling teachers, in that we were furnished with the underpinning socio-psychological theory that affects how pupils learn and behave. They were rarely called students then, that term being reserved for post-18 education where learning and research was as much the individual's own responsibility under tutorial guidance. Pupil learning in schools was largely prescriptive. Pupils followed either GCE (General Certificate in Education) courses, taken by the top 10% - mainly those who had passed an exam at 11 years old and had won place at a Grammar School, or CSE (Certificate in Secondary Education) ones for the remainder in a Secondary Modern School. Exams in both 'pathways' demanded factual regurgitation and rote learning of teacher-given notes. There was little opportunity for individual evaluation and/or reasoned self-opinion, and limited flexibility for any interchange between the two prescriptive curriculums.

We student teachers were also well versed in the preparation and use of non-IT, i.e. primitive and basic, 'audio visual aids' such as loading and working a slide projector. In fact, most of us, fuelled by cereals and fast food, boarded public transport weighed down with various bulky teaching aids on our way to our designated practice schools.

Back then sticks of coloured chalk were coveted and certainly not handed out in packs to student teachers of the here today, gone tomorrow, brigade. Nowadays a memory stick (or an email to the school) and a link to the classroom interactive white board would add so much more multi-sensory interest and stimulation, not to mention being that much easier to prepare.

However, classroom discipline was rarely discussed on the university course and the responsibility for this seemed to be very much up to each individual. Practical classroom elements relating to this, such as where in the room to stand and/or sit, when and how to project your voice and even how to write on a blackboard, were never mentioned, so they were never discussed. Writing neatly and in horizontal lines on a board is not as easy as it might appear.

At first my efforts were like a short-sighted doctor's own

Our tutors expected us to initiate pupil-centred learning involving as many of the class as possible in debate and discussion, avoiding being merely dispassionate purveyors of facts. We were told that we, as fledgling teachers, should not lecture but encourage guided self-discovery amongst our pupils. We were told that we should act as if we were 'the guide by the side' and not 'the sage on the stage.' Any bad behaviour and/or under achievement was most likely due to poverty, deprivation, disillusionment, lack of opportunities or a dearth of relevant curriculum themes, or a combination of them all – none of which, as temporary teachers, we could do much about. The issue of confronting and dealing with bad behaviour in the classroom and the school campus was also skirted around, so ignoring the most challenging aspect of day-to-day teaching, i.e. classroom management. In fact, most of us weren't clear where the appropriate or acceptable dividing line should be drawn; on reflection it's probably about personal standards and tolerance.

The odd part about trying to create a safe, calm environment in which all pupils can learn is that once you have set the scene, the cast, characters and plot constantly change; what works in one class doesn't necessarily succeed in another. It's about adapting yourself to the personality of the class as a whole.

Other advice could have been useful; for example,

teach noticeably better than your seniors whilst taking an overt interest in their methods and converse more with the positive members of staff, politely dismissing the serial moaners. The latter are usually the ageing, embittered individuals who have missed out on promotion more than once. It was with these ideals in mind that our first element of two six-week stints of teaching practice began, i.e. a week of classroom observation of teaching in a local primary school. I was apprehensive to say the least, and certainly naïve.

So, come the first day, I arrived at my allocated primary school in a South Wales valley, prepared to see how it should be done. Even though most of our university cohort were preparing to be secondary teachers, primary *observation*

for the first week was compulsory. As I was sitting in the staffroom aware of both sympathy and distant disdain, especially after initially sitting in the 'wrong' chair and drinking tea from 'someone else's' cup, the Headmaster found me. To my utter horror he informed me that I could, if I wanted, take Mrs K's class of seven-year-olds for morning lessons, as she was ill and would be a last-minute absentee. I was petrified. What sort of university reference would I get if I refused?

"What should I teach them?" I enquired, as calmly as my fear would allow.

"Read them a story," he replied.

At that moment I could only think of Rupert Bear for some reason; perhaps because I enjoyed those adventures as a child.

"I'll get you a book" he reassuringly continued. This was a gentle dive into the deep end.

It went as well as could be expected, though the reading was punctuated by question and answer sessions, most of which ended with personal queries – their curiosity was unbounded in that respect. "Are you English/married/a student/a school inspector visiting, so we have to be quiet?" they variously asked. I tried my best to be professionally evasive.

I was also expected to help with games lessons which, in this part of the country for the boys at any rate, meant rugby. The Headmaster was an enthusiastic coach of the sport and asked if I could "take the stragglers" as he'd heard that I was a fan of the round ball game; I don't think he could bring himself to use either of the words 'football' or 'soccer' in that context. Just then, one of the boys, who had recently arrived from across the border, said "Are we playing rugger today sir?" to which the Head replied scathingly "No boy, only English homosexuals play rugger. We will be playing Rugby Football."

During his enthusiastic coaching of the basics of rugby, young lads would often come up from a scrum bemoaning the effect of packing down on their ears and/or neck. They would promptly be pushed down again with their ears now ringing as well, with the words "Nobody should be uncomfortable in the scrum, lad".

Following the observational week, I was informed that because of my academic background, for the next week I would start teaching about the atmosphere, beginning with air. At the time, given that it is invisible, tasteless and odourless, it did not seem the most tangible of topics to take on with six and seven-year-olds. I was given a text to base the lessons on and began with feathers rising over a hot radiator – until a small girl said "My mum says I'm allergic to feathers." I discreetly asked her to stand at the furthest point from the radiator, and carried on without further mishap.

Following that, things went better than I had expected and I enjoyed teaching these young ones, though the staffroom banter was a world away from that of the students' union; bringing back capital punishment, even for relatively trivial offences, was roundly endorsed and that room, even by the standards of the 1970s, was not exactly a hotbed of political correctness. Apart from the Headmaster, the teaching staff were all female; was the male of the species not welcome in the world of primary education?

My subsequent secondary school teaching practice in a large local comprehensive was more demanding, not least because specialist subject tutors would arrive unannounced and sit in the lesson to assess you and your written lesson planning where you have attempted to justify your approach to the topic being taught (methodology) and subsequently have to evaluate the relative success of the lesson. Rather daunting in all, especially the staff room, where I managed to sit in the 'wrong' chair again – a padded one, more comfortable than the rest, which looked like they'd come from a forerunner of IKEA.

Teaching across the age range (from juniors, year 7 up, and including GCE 'A' level) had to be seen by the tutor in my assigned secondary school, a large urban comprehensive. Although I was saturated with idealism, I didn't want to be seen by staff or pupils as some kind of trendy milksop.

My particular junior class (third year, or year 9 as it would be now) were a mixed-ability class of largely charming individuals who were fascinated by my 'foreign' accent and relative youth. They appeared to listen with curiosity to my reasons as to why Japanese companies had located in South Wales recently – my given teaching topic. However, a class walkabout whilst they were writing off the board revealed mixed ability to be an understatement. With 10 minutes of lesson time left, some had completed the follow-up extension questions, whilst others had nowhere near finished even copying my introductory writing off the board. It would be unfair to set homework as 'finish off' as the less able would have too much and the more able would be left unstretched. This would have to be included in my lesson evaluation and rectified before the second tutorial visit of this class, which turned out to be two days later, as I had anticipated. I had 'briefed' the class on the tutor's impending visit, explaining as much as I needed to, and one boy said genuinely "Shall we stand up when he comes in?" Immediately, without thinking, I said "Yes." The tutor duly arrived, introduced by the Head of Department, and amidst a screeching of chairs they all stood up. My tutor was impressed and the Head of Department was stunned and briefly dumbfounded. "They've never done that before," she whispered to me as the tutor took his customary position at the back of the classroom. She left with a grin, muttering to herself in Welsh.

This lesson was a follow-up to the introductory one on Japanese industrial location in South Wales, ensuring some continuity from the previous one, so avoiding any possible confusion or distraction. It went really well, with keen hands rising to answer questions. Unfairly, I had, however, already mentally earmarked which hands to choose for what I'd hoped would be reasonably rational responses. I had also manipulated the class seating arrangements so that the brightest pupils sat at the back and sides of the room near the tutor's 'perch.' In this way if the tutor leaned from his position at the back to look at their exercise books, things would reflect well on me. Unfortunately, he walked all around the room, casually looking at a cross-section of written work which revealed a huge disparity, both in quantity and quality. This was discussed later during a debrief, and I explained it away by saying that I had heard from the staff that they were a class consisting of one of the widest ranges of mixed ability in the school. I didn't consider my tutor the best person to advise me on this, as I knew that he had only ever taught at Manchester Grammar School – one of the most selective and elitist educational institutions in the country.

This spell also involved shadowing a Head of Year undertaking a lunchtime duty across the campus, making sure that acceptable behaviour was the norm outside the classroom too. A recurring problem seemed to be unsaddled, untethered horses and ponies wandering all over the school playing fields. I was informed that these were ridden bareback to school by gypsy children, the majority of whom were quickly gathered together at lunchtime and told in no uncertain terms that the establishment would not tolerate these animals 'fouling school grounds'.

At the end of each exhausting week, we trainee practitioners would take solace in the student union bar, taking communal comfort from the shared commiserations of lessons that had not gone exactly to plan. An alcoholic debrief, I suppose. Retrospective reflections on teaching practice weeks were always conducted in the bar on a Friday evening and most of the discussion centred on classroom discipline; it was mutually agreed that much of our lecturers' advice and preparation in this respect could be considered dubious, peripheral or even inadvisable. Sarcasm, we were told, should be avoided, but there seemed a consensus of opinion that if it was delivered with the utmost sincerity, it could be a useful tool; somebody even used the word 'weapon'. Mystery was also useful; telling pupils little about yourself stretched and maintained their curiosity – if not for the topic taught, then for you yourself. Keep your private life just that. We also learnt that having been thrown in the deep end, we tended to be gullible. If word got around that you were a student teacher, you were fair game. An experience common to many of us in those early days was a boy knocking on the door asking if a particular pupil could see the Headteacher. Without further questioning, the child involved would be released and the two pupils would shortly be seen running across the playing fields, like escaped convicts, for a day off – as happened to one of us 'greenhorns'.

Dropping the name of the Head of Year into the conversation occasionally was also useful, especially if he or she was a figure of fear and respect; or, as one of the students in a more 'demanding' school was told by an experienced hand, get a list of the 'frighteners' on the staff. In a similar vein, another student, when asking a senior member of staff's advice, was told to get a list of the 'potential troublemakers' (preferably with mugshots) in each class beforehand so that he could identify them early in the lesson and nip any misbehaviour in the bud. Other 'off course' suggestions included intimating that you may have spent time at Her Majesty's Pleasure at some stage, not disclosing any details, whilst mentioning this to another of the teaching staff so you had back up and 'street cred'.

Despite academics assuring us to the contrary, pupil appearances, it was generally agreed, were *not* deceptive. Extreme haircuts, earrings (even in those days) and only a passing nod to the school uniform usually marked out potential miscreants. If they were challenging the uniform, it was likely that they would challenge the teaching staff too.

It now seems common sense that any teacher should demonstrate absolute control of a class from the start, including the careful lining up of pupils in the corridor first, maintaining order and quiet before they are even admitted (in order of queuing) into in the room, but we disgruntled students had not been told that beforehand. It was learning on the job in more ways than one.

Some students had made the mistake of talking to the pupils in 'yoofspeak', trying to be trendy friendly on their level, and this did not work, as you are not there to be their friend, only to be friendly.

One piece of sound advice from the course, though much disputed at the time, was to dress smartly. It works! Forget all this 'dressing down' with the kids; they respect a smart appearance, especially a suit, which often make them assume that you're more important than is actually the case. Similarly, with the pupils, you soon learn to insist that everyone wears every item of their school uniform correctly. Nowadays, with interactive whiteboards, teaching attire no longer gets covered in chalk dust.

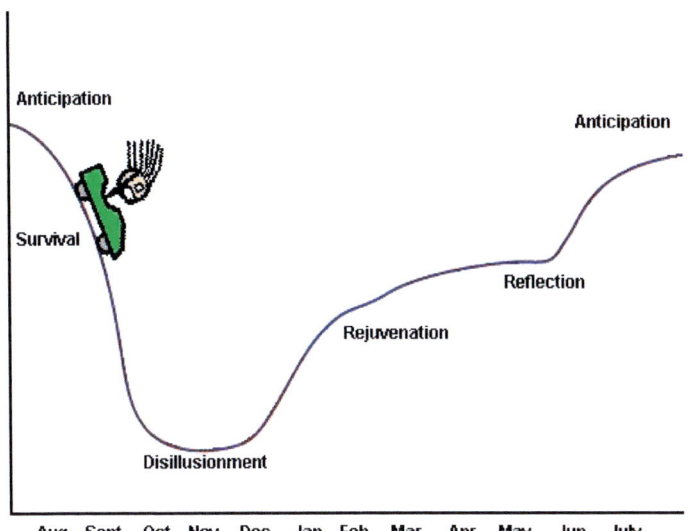

Further lesson preparations for the future and evaluations of the past could then be forgotten for a couple of evenings after this student union communal offload.

The course eventually finished with the presentation of a dissertation and one student – we will call him F – had been somewhat less than diligent with previous work deadlines, spending more time in the bar than in the library. However, with this final piece of written work he had apparently finished at 9pm for the 9am deadline the following day and wanted everyone to know that. So, presumably after imbibing in the bar since 9pm, he had staggered back to the halls of residence somewhere around 1am, attaché case in hand, urging everyone to wake up at the top of his voice and shouting "It's all in here" (referring to the contents of his case). He was standing unsteadily in a central lawned area at the time and ended up being covered in raw eggs and far worse thrown from the adjacent rooms by agitated occupants whom he had woken up.

I now realised that children were going to be the raw material of my career and that successfully managing a class of hormonal teenagers would only come with experience. Career advancement within the profession was something else that was not touched on by the PGCE course. It appeared from practice that you needed to impress not only the Head, but those on the staff who appeared stronger with both colleagues and pupils.

Chapter 2

Into the real world

Being a southerner, I had decided to apply for any jobs south of a line from Bristol to London at any school that offered both of my subjects on the curriculum; unusual at that time. At this point I still had the following ringing in my ears: "Roughly speaking education gets tougher as you go further north. Scotland's addiction to flagellation worried the Cadogan committee…" (Price, 1960, p.69. This refers to a report commissioned by the Government in 1938 to investigate corporal punishment in schools.)

At an exhaustive interview that included the local butcher/governor as part of the panel, I decided to direct my answers to the Chairman of the Governors, as the others seemed to defer to him. After a grilling, I was accepted for a post in a large (1500-plus) comprehensive school in the south east. I was given a decent flat at a peppercorn rent by the local 'New Towns' council – supposedly to entice 'professionals' into this modern settlement.

The school was situated in the more affluent part of town, which meant that its catchment area was dominated by residents of a higher socio-economic status with motivated parents naturally having high expectations of their offspring and those that taught them. Needless to say, parents' evenings were well attended. No pressure then.

My Head of Department was an affable middle-aged man, appearing somewhat detached from the rest of his 'team.' I was soon to learn that he was literally moonlighting, earning extra, possibly untaxed, income from lorry driving at night! 'Informal employment' would be a euphemism for this type of work. He was reputed to have said, according to one department member, that each extra mile on the clock brought retirement from teaching a day nearer. This additional 'responsibility' may help to explain why he registered a girl in his tutor group present on the first day of the year when the family had moved to Scotland the previous summer. He had missed the pre-term staff meeting an hour earlier when this fact was announced. A member of the secretarial staff collating the registers had picked up on this. However, as part of my probationary year assessment, he passed my 'inspected lesson' without much ado – partly, I suspect, because it meant less work for him.

The Headmaster here very occasionally used the cane as a means of punishment and deterrent. From what I could gather the mental torture of waiting in the corridor outside his office was far more agonising than the physical pain inflicted. This continued once inside, where canes were hung on hooks in rows in a glass cabinet on the wall (which could be seen through his window). If the blind was down, other pupils assumed the worst for one of their own. A well-rehearsed routine then ensued whereby each cane was slowly tested for length, thickness and flexibility in front of the miscreant. The final deed was then recorded in a battered black, leather-bound, book which presumably had been thwacked repeatedly in testing.

The Deputy Headmaster was nicknamed 'Gandhi' by the pupils because of an obvious facial resemblance, but there the similarities ended. He certainly was not a pacifist and both staff and pupils quaked at the thought of being summoned by him; he dealt with serious disciplinary measures with apparent relish.

On the subject of discipline, as with teaching practice, most of the more memorable and occasionally amusing incidents arose outside the classroom but within the confines of the campus. An illustration would again be a lunchtime duty, patrolling the corridors ensuring reasonable behaviour within the buildings out of class time.

My second turn at this saw a middle school pupil (year 4/5 or 10/11 now) temporarily bandage his fist with a soft-back book and, encouraged and egged on by his mate, thrust the said fist through a glass door panel. Having turned to see me many metres down the long corridor, they fled and the bell rang for afternoon lessons.

I followed this up with the Head of Year the following day. Now this man was an intimidating physical presence (an ex-wrestler, it was whispered) – a factor no doubt relevant to his appointment. I told him I would recognise the said miscreant but, as I did not teach him, I couldn't name him. We agreed to meet in his room at lunch-time where, as far as I could gather, I would be presented with an identity parade of likely suspects which ultimately turned out to be three, presumably based on my descriptions and his knowledge of the pupils with 'past form.' The culprit was immediately identified and the others initially dismissed.

Then something incredible happened. I was picked from the floor by my shoulders by the Head of Year and physically carried upright like a soldier to attention, with profuse apologies proffered, and asked to stand against the back wall of the room. The room door was then wedged open and the boy told to bend over just inside the door entrance. Our pastoral educationalist then left to walk down about three metres down the corridor that led off his room. Then, taking what must have been a size 11 plimsoll out of the inside of his jacket pocket, he explained that he was going to 'slipper' the boy, but needed a run-up in order for it to be more effective, and my previous position would have impeded that!

The boy, who was now nearer to me, was, not surprisingly, sweating profusely (so was I, mildly) during the deliberate, presumably well-rehearsed, delay. He carried out all this to the word and the boy was dismissed. As far as I am aware, he gave no trouble after that.

Whatever the rights and wrongs of corporal punishment, the school was exceedingly well run and, after comparing notes with friends elsewhere, I realised I had landed on my feet. Unlike teaching practice, I was here in front of the class by right and no longer a temporary student teacher.

The teaching staff here did much for the pupils outside of the curriculum, running numerous sports teams and various other clubs unpaid. Interestingly, no mention was made during the PGCE course of the significance and importance that running out-of-school activities makes in a teacher's career advancement. I took a cricket team there in the light of the above and looked to establish myself as an invaluable, but not threatening, member of the school community.

Another career advancement option would be to...

...marry a Headmaster's daughter.

Staff here also put on a Christmas show into which I was press-ganged. The general theme was the 'Tamla Motown Years', which were less distant then. I was to be one of Diana Ross's Supremes. While this involved simple miming (or lip-synching now) to 'Baby Love', there was a more intricate dance routine to learn in a long, tight, sparkly dress – and to l earn quickly during after-school rehearsals. The advantage of the outfit was that only the hands, face and upper neck had to be blacked up. Maybe political correctness would have prevented that now. The said routine involved two stools around which we were supposed to pirouette and not drag; they should have been nailed to the floor, but there were other 'acts' to follow. The word 'choreography' was never mentioned.

Backstage there was a whiff of apprehension, trepidation and whisky in the air immediately beforehand. However, I have never been the recipient of such collective, thunderous, appreciative applause and screaming before or since as that which greeted us after the performance. Our disguises were but paper-thin and word soon got around as to who the real personae were behind each act. It made subsequent teaching easier, as the pupils had seen us in a different light, having appreciated that we were prepared to make fools of ourselves on stage as well as in the classroom. I hoped that I was giving the impression of job devotion, while remaining human. I made certain however that I watched some television as, in those days, with no internet and mobile phones, I would have little other point of social contact and conversation with the pupils I taught.

One teacher there, keen for career 'advancement' and having decided that there were no departmental opportunities for her possible 'promotion', invented a post of responsibility to further her cause; that of 'bicycle (shed) monitor.' She wrote several sides of A4 detailing the necessity of this role at the end of the school day when there was a rush to cycle home, and forwarded it to the Head, who promptly refused on the grounds that there had been no problems or safety issues with this in the past. In addition, an incremental point on the salary scale for a job that probably warranted all of 30 minutes a day and one which a lollipop lady could do was not a high priority. There are times when ambition needs to be coated with at least a veneer of realism.

It was here that a female laboratory assistant had an instant dose of realism. This particular individual gave every appearance of being a strict disciplinarian and was very vocal in criticising both teachers and parents who she felt were too lenient with their charges. That was until her daughter, in year 10, was found to be giving boys 'sexual favours' for cash on the school campus during school time. The assistant resigned the same term. People in glass houses...

It was unofficially confirmed by the school that I had passed my probationary year, so I was deemed acceptable to be let loose on the secondary sector at large. In the light of this I had already decided to move on and farther west, as I knew the area well, having been brought up there. I was making job applications in these areas.

During the year I had made good friends with a Maths teacher, J, and we socialised regularly. J had a teaching room overlooking the tennis courts. Towards the end of the teaching year the school was a focus for teaching practice for girls from a nearby specialist PE teacher-training college. Two girls were coaching some pupils in tennis below J's teaching room on the last day of the summer term and therefore the end of the academic year; they did not go unnoticed by him. At the end of school he casually informed me that *we* were taking them out for a drink that evening!

All went well, including their acceptance of a coffee back at J's flat. However, as soon as we all got through the front door he took me aside and in hushed tones, bordering on panic, he told me to take them into the kitchen, make the coffee and keep them 'amused' until he came back in. Eventually, after emptying our cups and disposing of his old pot noodle cartons, confused and baffled, I left the girls to go into his lounge to find out what was going on; after all, I hardly knew them. There, in the lounge which appeared to double as a darts room, I found J manically kicking what could only be loosely described as magazines of a risqué nature under the couch and chairs. "OK, it's fine to come in now," he said.

Chapter 3

A year's supply teaching

After leaving the South East I moved nearer home and found a supply job teaching my own subject, covering for a long-term staff absence, at a local Secondary Modern school with its first year of a comprehensive intake. In many ways it was like teaching practice, only with more experience; you weren't ultimately responsible for their exam results and future careers and were not expected to get involved in extra-curricular activities. So, all in all, limited accountability. However, whilst there is less pressure in relation to exam results, there are a number of drawbacks to longer-term supply. In those days a teacher had little warning of when and where you were required on supply, never mind what you were required to teach. You would just get a phone call in the morning from a school where someone had reported in sick for the day and, without the internet, you had little access to knowledge of the establishment itself, including its exact location.

Entering the staffroom for the first time was a fraught business; there were usually all sorts of protocols that you were unaware of, and each school was different in that respect. Previous experience made me apprehensive of sitting in the wrong chair or worse still, drinking from the wrong mug. Also, more often than not the absentee teacher you were covering for had set no work; either that or it had been set, but nobody could find out where it was! Similarly, text books and exercise books were not always to hand. The classroom was somebody else's castle and you were but a temporary occupant.

It was here that I was advised unofficially that there was a full-time post in the offing at the end of the year and it was strongly intimated by the Headmaster that I should apply. He told me that he would have to advertise the post, but the job was mine if I wanted it; the Deputy Head, however, also a teacher in the same department, told me *not* to apply. Apparently the absentee Head of Department, who I was covering for, had repeatedly feathered her own nest in making sure she alone taught the more able and better behaved classes. That was why it had gone well then. The Deputy Head further informed me, in the strictest professional confidence that I, as an NQT (Newly Qualified Teacher), would be given those classes that she herself did not fancy teaching. The post he suggested would be more of a test of my teaching technique than any academic ability or preference; more of a long-term minder of lower ability classes.

Once the above Head of Department returned, I managed to obtain another long supply post at a local Secondary Modern, teaching various subjects using work set. Here I found a rather demotivated, disaffected staff and pupils, nearly all of whom had to share outdated textbooks in class and were not allowed to take any out, giving staff a 'reason' not to set homework and therefore limit corrective marking and workload. I didn't have to oversee any Maths lessons, but I imagined the subject being taught with a rusty abacus in one of the damp, mouldy, musty prefabs.

These pupils had failed the old, largely defunct, 11-plus exam to determine the kind of curriculum they would follow and felt they were on the academic scrapheap. Worse still, their teachers felt under no pressure to stretch them academically as they weren't, in their minds, the ablest anyway. Also, many had siblings who *had* passed the 11-plus and were accommodated in a new, purpose-built grammar school just down the road, and this was well equipped and resourced for both academic and extra-curricular activities. Everybody there had a textbook they could take home to work from and their huge playing fields were not being diminished by the erection of prefabs. Those secondary modern pupils were the best argument against the return of grammar schools.

During this period I was invited for what turned out to be an informal interview at a senior independent school. The interview was unusual in that there was no intimidating panel of interviewers – just the Head. There was no Deputy Head and no representatives from the governing body to form the usual dreaded crescent facing you. Previous interview panels had included the butcher, baker and candlestick-maker from the governing body, each of whom read what appeared to be individually pre-allocated questions at set points during the procedure. They then listened to the responses without appearing to comprehend them, as they were delivered in a professional language they had rarely encountered. School governors then were usually well-meaning pillars of the local community, with but with a child's experience of school education. But this time there was just the Head, sitting cross-legged in a large chair with his legs under him like a small Buddha, and we talked about almost everything except education. That discussion was left to the existing Head of Department on a walkabout, with me dressed like an applicant for a junior managerial post – dressed up, but not in my best suit, which had last been worn at a funeral.

I was impressed by the well-manicured lawns and playing fields, not to mention the sandstone buildings of the frontage, which included a marvellous chapel, complete with stained glass windows. This compared very favourably with the graffiti and litter-strewn red brick Victorian school of my secondary teaching practice.

I was offered the post and accepted.

Chapter 4

Working in the independent sector

Early days

This post was a culture shock for me in more ways than one. For a start, the school had only just embarked on a policy of admitting girls after the best part of a hundred years, although there were just a handful in the Sixth Form when I started, so it could barely be called mixed at this stage. Because of the large majority of males there was a degree of sexism amongst those boy pupils, especially when staff referred to girls by their given names (the boys were traditionally called by their surnames), leading to accusations of favouritism.

There was no bell or buzzer to signal the beginning and

end of lessons, which was very civilised and less manic all round. Term names were different too; Michaelmas and Lent replacing the more usual seasonal names, paying lip service to religion.

It was also a boarding school with about a third of the school attendees 'in house'. Every potential pupil applying to the school had to sit an entrance exam testing basic literacy, logic and numeracy. It was a case of financial supply and demand; with a large 'surplus' of applicants the school could be more selective, ensuring a more able intake. However, boarding places had to be filled for economic reasons, and it was often apparent that boarders were, on average, less able than the average day pupil. In those days many of the boarders were the offspring of service personnel who, on account of being frequently moved around, could have a percentage of the fees paid by the government.

Boarding staff or housemasters (every teacher was a 'master' then) were somewhat institutionalised, having spent the best part of their lives in the 'care' of the school. During term time, every meal was provided for them – and very good food it was too. Every whim was catered for, boarding staff eating in their own private dining room, served before the rest of the teachers and being waited on by kitchen staff who folded their red serviettes into water tumblers. They could also remain on site during the school holidays, but had to feed themselves.

Several of the more senior housemasters were imbued with the notion that most of the world's problems were a consequence of the disintegration of the British Empire and us joining the Common Market, as it was known then. The French were characterised as unhygienic, serial white flag-waving surrenderists and the Germans as humourless, inveterate, imperial expansionists – all in Fawltyish asides that were underpinned by more than a veneer of xenophobia. God knows whether their charges heard all this in those days of political incorrectness, with all the implied racism.

One housemaster was an absolute authority on local public transport, never having driven a car. In pre-internet days most teaching staff would contact him if there was any doubt about local bus and train times; he'd memorised the lot, including seasonal and weekend deviations. One unfortunate housemaster of a boys' boarding house seemed to need adult company in his social life and often invited staff around for an evening drink or several – usually of whisky. His need for alcohol stemmed apparently from the sudden departure of his wife for another woman. Perhaps she objected to his pipe-smoking habit (it was banned later on the campus) and in particular the frequent rubbing of the bowl along the side of his nose before relighting. In time, with the school becoming mixed from the top down, husband and wife 'teams' took over boarding house responsibilities, replacing several life-long bachelors.

Many of the day staff thought that any housemaster who had to combine the responsibilities of a prison warder, zoo-keeper and amateur psychiatrist with those of a teacher could hardly be expected to be 'normal.' It was a 24/7 *in loco parentis* job in term time, after all.

At this time I was staying in a bed and breakfast near the school; the same one where I had spent the night before my interview. However, my room now was nowhere near as comfortable as the first one and the better ones seem to be reserved for the season's tourists. I hadn't previously noticed the landlady's notice of dos and don'ts which included 'no female visitors unless they are relatives' and a rule that anyone returning after 10:30 had to give her prior notice and enter via the tradesman's entrance at the rear of the building! Also the bathroom/toilet had to be accessed along a damp, carpeted landing and the notice on the door proudly announced that hot water was available from 7am to 9am and from 5pm to 9pm. I didn't stay long there.

At this early time in the independent sector, respect from the pupils was assumed and did not, for the most part, have to be earned; pupils always stood up when you entered the classroom. In the majority of secondary schools nowadays the class would not be allowed into the classroom before the teacher's arrival and on their say-so, for fear of potentially bad behaviour and possible risk of damage to the fabric of the room, or even the building.

Compared to my experience in the state sector the

school was comparatively small – fewer than 750 pupils – and there appeared to be little PR or motivation for increasing that. Getting to know both pupils and staff was therefore easier. There was an informal, friendly atmosphere which, for the best part, was welcome, but there was no pupil disciplinary structure or mechanism in place. Bad behaviour could initially be reported to form tutors and ultimately the Headmaster, who would often merely tell the pupil to apologise to the individual who had first reported the incident. There were no pastoral heads of year to act as a deterrent as, I suspect, the school felt that the general behaviour was good enough not to warrant such posts.

The average age of the staff was much higher than I'd previously experienced. Staff came and stayed; a sign of a less taxing establishment. There was also an atmosphere of restrained eccentricity there. Of course this was in the days before league tables and exam results accountability, when non-teaching time equated with an assumed period of relaxation. Some Heads of Department even had interesting sidelines that you felt they'd rather be attending to, e.g. cultivation of strawberries in one case and worms ('red wigglers' apparently) in another. Others concentrated on their teaching – even if it meant standing on a chair to gain the pupils' attention, as an elderly classics teacher managed to frequently do. It seemed like something out of a Tom Sharpe novel – especially *Vintage Stuff*.

Yet another Head of Department, H, felt it necessary to correct the spelling and punctuation of every sports board notice pinned up in one of the main corridors, in red ink. This particular individual also had a problem with spatial awareness and would frequently bump into colleagues and pupils in such corridors without apparently noticing and with no word of apology. (This may have been because his eyes seemed to operate independently of each other.) H's car was testament to this, with numerous dents and sub-parallel scratches down both sides. Even on a campus where parking was at a premium, his car was given a wide berth by colleagues and there was usually a deliberately vacant space either side of his vehicle. The same person also ran the school library in my early days and was meticulous, bordering on OCD, in both the cataloguing (according to the Dewey system of course) and shelf - stacking of books for loan and reference. Of course the pupils picked up on this and books would be deliberately moved into sections that had no bearing on their subject matter. Also, magazines of an adult nature were inserted into the section taught by this person, sending him into a fit of apoplectic rage amid barely-stifled sniggering from behind tall stacks of shelves. His eventual replacement, a trained librarian, thankfully restored efficient normality. H was also a keen tennis player in his younger days, but in the one appearance on court witnessed by his colleagues he looked like an extra from *Chariots of Fire*. I remember the very same man stood totem-still in the quad whilst his Sixth Form teaching set did an end of term circular conga around him.

Another, more senior, Head of Department used his own university lecture notes to teach 'A' Level; they were so old that the paper was wrinkled and the edges stained brown with foxing, almost resembling the Dead Sea scrolls – and that in a diurnally dynamic subject.

Other acts of apparent eccentricity took place off campus. One Head of Department drove to London, only to forget where he had parked his car, forcing him to take the train back. Whilst on the subject of off-campus and cars, in my early years I was given a lift into school by an RE teacher who lived near me. His driving was erratic to say the least and certainly lacking in any awareness of roundabout procedure or etiquette. He would drive right across them without looking, just smiling at those who were screaming obscenities at him. He had a joker playing card pinned to his dashboard, apparently to remind him that most other drivers could not be taken seriously. He was somewhat lacking in crowd control with his classes and although they did well in school exams (he gave them the questions beforehand), their external results were much worse. For those reasons, later timetabling was tailored to his limitations rather than his needs, in that he was given junior, non-external exam teaching.

It has to be remembered that in those days there was no national curriculum and for the first three years, before

GCE 'O' Level teaching, Heads of Department could choose whatever subject matter they thought appropriate for their staff to teach in those early years. The above teacher was however frequently timetabled in the room next to mine and, whilst there was audible bedlam in his room, he would frequently leave his class and pop in for a chat about anything other than education.

Ironically, the RE teacher who replaced the above man when he retired suffered similar issues. In her first year at school she set the internal third year exam just as her predecessor had. This time, however, instead of giving them the questions, she brought the paper in to give them revision hints, as promised the previous lesson. At this point an 'office runner' came into her class with 'an urgent message' from the 'Head's secretary' – except there wasn't one. A less naive member of staff put her right, but only when her exam results had far exceeded those of the other third year forms. Yes, the pupils had snapped the question paper, left in haste, with a mobile phone while she was out of the room and it found its way to most members of the form. Yet her form's GCSE uptake was very small despite those 'outstanding' results in the school exam!

What with this, and paint brushes and other materials flying out of the window of the art room below and onto the rose bed while the Head of Department was actually teaching, I wondered what I had let myself in for. Perhaps the art teacher was subconsciously preparing the border as an entry for the Turner Prize. I don't think the school caretaker who occasionally weeded the beds had such an esoteric take on their appearance. Either way, the stench of glue, paint, white spirit and what smelt like burning polystyrene was palpable and sickly.

Teaching then was a very conservative profession and tended to equate experience with duration. The Head of Art was a senior member of staff and I hadn't been in the game long.

One particular senior teacher had a striking resemblance to 'Chalkie', the teacher in many a Giles cartoon (below). Many of his colleagues had surreptitiously remarked on this, though it went largely unnoticed by the pupils, who presumably, and perhaps understandingly, were not au fait with old issues of the *Daily Express*.

The school had a member of the clergy on the staff. He was responsible for the pastoral care of pupils and occasionally the staff, in addition to some teaching of RE and occasional local preaching in the community. One particular incumbent had a fondness for whisky and was often seen imbibing in the town, where he would occasionally visit a local nightclub 'after hours', and that was where two younger members of staff happened upon him one Saturday night. He, like most others in the club, was viewing that night's entertainment (some female mud wrestling) from a balcony. When the Chaplain was asked what he thought of it by the two younger members of staff, he replied, between puffs on his pipe, "I've seen better!"

This person, as part of his professional remit, was also occasionally required to 'baby sit' boarding pupils to give the Housemaster a midweek break. Quite why he needed one of the dinner ladies to help him with that one evening remains a mystery. The same individual Chaplain was also the root cause of an exasperated and vociferous outburst from the Bursar overheard by many in the corridor; apparently his landline bill, for which the school was responsible, was well in excess of what could be expected for reasonable pastoral conversation and care within the school community. Whilst no member of the teaching staff had seen a confirmatory, corroborating invoice, it was rumoured that the excess was the result of him phoning sex chat lines in the United States – as part of his global pastoral remit, no doubt. The individual concerned left prematurely – apparently by reciprocal arrangement.

The above two younger teachers also visited another local night club where they were served cocktails by a 'bunny girl' who looked vaguely familiar; after a period of mental lag time they realised she was a girl in the Sixth Form. Nothing was said about this at school by any of the parties. Presumably her pocket money was insufficient.

Another RE teacher had a fascination with road kill. Frequently he would walk the lanes around his home, often at night, looking for dead wildlife either to eat or to stuff. Decision-making on delicacy or taxidermy must have been

"Oh boy! Have they got Chalkie's number! 'The teaching profession has been undermined by the convention that you cannot get rid of those who are incompetent or, worse still, positively dangerous.'"

guided by smell and state of preservation. This person also kept a corked ceramic pot on his classroom desk and shook it violently, producing a rattling noise, if any pupil failed to hand in homework. The rattling was the sound of fingernails which he kept in the jar, and when the pot was turned around it said clearly 'Taken From Homework Dodgers.'

This man also had such a distrust of his subject's external examiners and their marking that he entered himself for one of the papers and subsequently demanded a post-result in depth enquiry for detailed feedback on his script. He did however have a wonderful gift with the English language and other staff often admired his very concise and sometimes pithy report comments. On a third form (year 9) boy who was somewhat disengaged, lacking in concentration and overly chatty, he wrote "He speaks often, but says little." On another boy in the same form who was somewhat lacking in stature, but very able and motivated, he remarked "A mighty atom!" A year 11 pupil's report once read "If the Bible is the mouthpiece of morals, his is the voicebox of the rest." He invariably avoided the clichés used by the rest of us; no "A good term's work" or "Satisfactory progress" for him.

Yet another RE teacher (why is it so often them?) had an obsessional fascination for World War II aircraft and related militaria, often reading through relevant magazines in class when he should have been teaching. He was born fractionally too late for call-up and that fact was commonly used to explain his intense hobby. Unfortunately, most of the above was known to generations of pupils who, after repeated requests, would successfully sidetrack him for whole lessons on the early role of the Fleet Air Arm or whatever, whilst the intended teaching of the New Testament syllabus never got off the ground. Pupils on a

Wednesday had particularly short shrift and poor value from him, as that was the day his aircraft magazine came out and enquiring minds were left to do exercises from a textbook for fear of detention. Some in fact received a punishment, even though they were absent, as he had not even looked up to see who was there and merely chose the name of a previous miscreant with 'form'.

This particular man was also extremely thrifty, and a number of pupils had noticed him trawling through many local jumble sales for clothes. It showed in his appearance of ill-fitting sleeveless beige or khaki sweaters and creaseless trousers worn at half mast.

Another teacher, a lay preacher but a physicist, was a truly Christian humanitarian and believed that every pupil was inherently good; all were God's children after all. When it came to discipline, he would take a boy into his 'prep' room, maniacally waving a cane in a gyratory motion around his head in front of the class as he went in after. He would then proceed to whack the cane against the wall three times and the pupil would re-emerge with a smile on his face and a wink of an eye. Sometimes there was a smirking queue pleading to be 'caned'. One can only imagine the prep room lined with weals on the wall like those made by carts on the streets of Pompeii.

One woodwork teacher did not have particularly good classroom crowd control, and this was concerning the school in view of the obvious safety issues. Things came to a head after the teacher fell through several partly-sawn rungs of a ladder needed to access wood supplies aloft. Outraged, he resigned on the day and later ran a DIY business in a local town, whilst the culprit was quickly expelled.

"I have a report that some of you undesirables have kidnapped our caretaker because he refuses to strike."
Daily Express, February 8th, 1979

We also had a senior classics teacher who often rode to school on a tandem, the back seat presumably occupied by his wife during more leisurely transport pursuits. I say 'ride' when, more often than not, he was seen pushing the thing. Downhill he resembled Biggles, with similar headgear, but instead of a scarf flying out from his neck it was a tie that looked as if it had been made from curtain material from an old people's home. This particular man unfortunately had a large, somewhat bent Roman nose and the pupils quickly related this to his taught subject. He had a habit of 'paddling' his hands at the start of a lesson to calm pupils down. Apparently, one bright summer's morning, he did this in front of a white screen in profile with his nose in silhouette and the laughter echoed around several classrooms. He was reflecting one of his nicknames, 'Beaky', in more ways than one. The other was 'Concorde' and apparently, before the teacher's late entry one day, a 5th former mimicked him in front of the class by stating "I will not tolerate insults like that flying around!"

Teaching here was quite relaxed, even though some of the fee-paying parents thought the institution was like an educational slot machine; if the fees were paid at the beginning then the exam certificates would drop out at the end, regardless of how able and/or diligent the pupil was. Because of the high parental expectation, it necessarily followed that any pupil who failed to live up to that expectation was 'failing' (below average in one or more subjects) because of the school. It could be anything other than the completely unpalatable/unacceptable lack of ability.

Many staff were nearing retirement at this point and the average age was certainly the highest of any staff room I had previously encountered. Napping in the staff room at lunchtimes was commonplace and occasionally a card with 'DNR' (Do Not Resuscitate) written on it was placed gently on a lap. Because a few staff had retired immediately prior to my starting there was an age gap between the older staff and those recently appointed, and there was a chasm between the attitudes, values and opinions of the contrasting age groups over a spectrum of issues. This may have been a consequence of age, but many of the more senior staff had never encountered state education, either as pupils themselves or as teachers, and had not completed any kind of probationary year as a consequence – this not being a pre-requisite to teach in the independent sector. In the staff room this was reflected in the seating arrangement, there being two distinct and separate clusters of chairs, with the older ones seated playing bridge and/or smoking, forming an inner cabal like a gentlemen's club, though slightly more animated. The younger teachers made do with the less comfortable chairs and were engaged in more enthusiastic discussion about pupils and upcoming extra-curricular activities they'd organised.

One senior teacher somewhat cynically remarked "What I lack in enthusiasm, I more than make up for in experience." Using his rationale, there presumably comes a mid-career equilibrium where the fine balance between experience and enthusiasm equate to being the most effective teacher.

The two age groups rarely communicated with each other. This divide seemed to extend to off-campus socialising too. I and another newly-appointed colleague went for a drink in a pub in the nearby town and a vaguely familiar figure approached us and said "You know this pub is for senior staff, don't you?" I said I didn't and bade him a good evening, or words to that effect. It was only then, and in a pub, that I belatedly realised how staffrooms were, and probably still are, so hierarchical –structured almost in a feudal way.

Staff 'sartorial elegance' (see later story about the 'Agony Aunt' column) at this time was dominated by coarse tweed, tank tops and flares that elsewhere in the community had been discarded many years ago, along with the day-to-day wearing of academic gowns that gave teachers some perceived intellectual kudos over their charges.

In addition to the age divide, some of the more senior staff didn't get on with each other, especially after political discussions, and on one occasion a book was thrown in the staff room, hitting its intended target on the head. Other staff did not see eye-to-eye with other teachers' partners. An evening concert of Andean music at school was attended by most teaching staff and their partners. One couple arrived late and were driving quite fast up the school drive to make up time, whilst another couple were walking back down, having parked. The husband of one of the teaching staff on foot tapped on the bonnet of the arriving car as it slowed down and said in a somewhat patronising tone "I say old chap, don't you think you're driving too fast?" at which an outstretched arm with a fist on the end shot out of the window 'like a boxing glove on a spring' – the recipient's wife's description – and punched him in the face.

Staff and partner get-togethers were sometimes fractious, often illuminating and occasionally funny. With the arrival of a new Headmaster, the teaching staff and partners were invited to an informal social evening in the staff room to enable the new incumbent to get to know faces outside 'normal' hours and in a more relaxed setting. A buffet and wine were provided. One particular couple, the wife being a psychiatrist, abstained from the latter on religious grounds and slowly became more detached from the noisier masses. Another member of the teaching staff did not abstain. He became increasingly irritated by the presence of the psychiatrist and thought he should introduce himself, via his colleague, her husband, to this lady. On his meandering approach to the other side of the room, some swore they could see the colour drain from the face of the husband, who knew of his colleague's volatility and unpredictability. Eventually an introduction was effected and a swaying member of staff said to the psychiatrist "What do you make of me, Dr. F?" She replied rather sheepishly in a cut glass accent "I think you're rather drunk." "Yes" he replied, "I'm as pissed as a fart."

So much for the cross-departmental, cordial benefits of extra-curricular on-site entertainment. There were however many staff parties both on and off site which were very convivial, some ending with naked swimming in a nearby pool. Of course these were times when the drink-driving laws and their implementation were more liberal

...more than a place where children are educated.

and the penalty for conviction less severe.

Another thing beyond my own experience was the presence of a lost property 'office' which at that time opened at least once a week for retrieval of mislaid items. This was a good idea, as there was a record kept of the time, date and exact location of each find. Items in 'temporary' storage included a multitude of odd shoes (did their owners hop home?), a bra, a box of cigars (for Dad?), various items of sports kit and latterly more mobile phones and watches than you would find in any high street shop. After a certain length of time had elapsed with no claimant, some items in good enough condition were given to charity. The room, it has to be said, had no windows or ventilation, so it did have an 'ambience' all of its own – probably down to the socks.

Modern times

As time went on the average age of the staff fell and the exam results improved further – largely, I suspect, because of the introduction of league tables and more detailed IT attainment analysis of exam performance results. The statistical term 'value added' was used after every summer's GCSE and 'A' Level results. This compared external exam results at GCSE with entrance exam scores of five years earlier to ascertain if pupils were performing according to their ability and whether they were under or over-achieving. All this was done by teaching set, so every member of the teaching staff was accountable and under the microscope. Departments as a whole were being compared to establish who was getting the best out of the pupils, and the whole thing became internally competitive, which was good for pupils and fee-paying parents alike. A similar approach was taken by comparing 'A' Level attainment with GCSE. All this was done historically too, with year-by-year comparisons. With competition between departments, especially at 'A' Level, some subjects would try and deter borderline GCSE candidates from taking the A' Level course by saying that their subject was 'highly academic' – both in class and on reports. Other departments, like Maths, having failed with that approach, taught the most complex parts of the syllabus (or specifications) in the very first class of the Sixth Form in the hope of 'weeding out' weaker candidates early on as they dropped the subject in favour of something else perceived to be easier.

During this period the school was slowly becoming more PR conscious and indeed more corporate and competitive, as some other similar independent schools were closing after experiencing financial problems.

It was noticeable with time that some subject departments appeared to take on a collective personality characteristic, although individual teachers were different in their approach and professional personae. The Maths Department was quietly confident and yet outwardly cautious, rarely visibly engaged in any marking – there was, after all, only one answer and it was always at the end of the textbook.

In contrast, the members of the English faculty were more extrovert, flamboyant, vociferous and, indeed, sometimes more volatile, as perhaps to be expected from individuals more grounded in drama. They appeared to spend a lot of time reading and marking pupils' work, as it was more subjective than Maths. One teacher always hummed while doing so; the higher the pitch, the better the quality of work.

The Craft, Design and Technology (once woodwork and metalwork) staff were more 'mainstream' by comparison, sober socially and more conventional in dress – certainly when compared to Art teachers. Science teachers seemed to be more relaxed and often eccentric, especially in the presence of pupils, cuddling, conversing and canoodling with life-size class skeletons in biology and referring to fossil specimens by 'given' names.

The Biology Department however had bucked the trend of replacing more senior, often retiring, expensive staff with younger, newly-qualified teachers. They had appointed a former Head of Department in an all-girls' school in the North East of England who clearly saw the job as a staging post into permanent retirement in the south, briefly feathering her retirement nest. It was soon noticed that she was not the most animated or enthusiastic of pedagogues, sitting

'The governors are confident that your mathematical teaching skills are every bit as good as Carol Vorderman's, Miss Winthrop – but there the resemblance must end.'

on her personally-cushioned chair, dictating notes for all classes. Laid back, yes – in an upright way; dynamic – no. This sedate approach may have been a combination of weight, lack of mobility, general health and/or attitude. Either way, she did not endear herself to the rest of the department or the rest of the staff, who barely knew her for her year in post as she was never seen in either the staff room or dining room. Both were some distance from the laboratories and this may have been significant.

One particular chemistry teacher, G, was of the 'old school' and his teaching motto was 'A good chemist is a tidy chemist.' This meant that he conducted virtually all the demonstrations himself with pupils rarely, if ever, being allowed to do them themselves for fear of leaving the laboratory untidy. Reagents were not stored alphabetically but by their position in the periodic table, ensuring some pupil difficulty in finding them. This element of OCD, as with H earlier, meant G was not particularly popular with staff or pupils, and when coursework data had to be obtained by the pupils themselves, he left the profession muttering about government meddling adversely affecting education in general and science in particular.

His pupils had always been merely dispassionate observers and were never allowed to be involved in practical, pupil-centred learning, gathering data and then ending with reasoned evaluation of their approach.

Individual foreign language teachers seemed to prefer

their own company in the staff room, though their sense of humour was tested one day by the 'office runner', a Sixth Former with a 'free' period designated to run important errands from the main office to anywhere and anyone in the school. A French teacher with a Sixth Form class was required, said the runner with a smile on his face, to pick up a large French letter from the main office immediately the lesson ended. The said letter was in fact a confirmation of his French exchange arrangements, but the saucy secretary had changed the request from 'a letter in French' to 'a French letter', thereby ensuring much amusement (and some wry speculation) throughout the Sixth Form in no time.

Whilst exam result comparisons kept most of the staff on their toes, a certain individual (R) who was appointed on a one-year contract was different; he repeatedly missed his early morning periods with a Sixth Form set. After discreet investigations it turned out that he was also undertaking a night shift at a local baker's! He was also found be at a bank some afternoons when, again, he should have been teaching a Sixth Form. I bumped into this man at a GCSE examiners' meeting in Essex, though he hadn't told the school he would be taking a couple of days off to be there; he avoided me for that period and it was never discussed on our return. Whilst his departmental head was not amused, R gained much kudos with the rest of the staff by enthusiastically directing the staff Christmas pantomime with competence, panache and flair, all in Christmas socks that were never a pair. Unfortunately, drama was not the subject he was supposed to be teaching. Pupils loved staff pantos of course – it was staff making a fool of themselves after all.

One particular teacher, not a true thespian as such but an enthusiastic 'amateur', was keen to be involved on stage. He became concerned about being typecast, usually playing the back end of a cow, so one year the role of a horse was somehow shoehorned into the script to placate him. The staff also put on a school play each year, though this, in many ways, resembled a pantomime under a different name.

Another member of the teaching staff also went AWOL on a teaching day and soon found himself in the local newspaper, as he had to be rescued from the sea at a distant beach in the afternoon.

With time, the ratio of males to females in both staff and pupils became lower and sexism was rare and the school the better for it, all pupils now being referred to by their given names. The girls were no longer regarded as a curiosity and did not have to be "bubbly, fluffy and confident" to fit in. (*The Times*, 1989, with reference to the early days of co-education at Charterhouse). However, even by the 1990s, female pupils were still a minority – their admission having started from the top (Sixth Form) down. A number of boys still felt that the girls received more favourable treatment, especially when it came to the appointment of prefects and leniency with respect to eccentricities of uniform. What is true is that a number of long-standing staff, only having taught boys for the best part of their lives, were somewhat uncomfortable in dealing with girls.

Of course the school, like the media, spent hours statistically comparing exam attainment at GCSE and 'A' Level by sex. This merely supported national trends in that girls do slightly better at GCSE, largely because of better prepared coursework, but by 'A' Level there is no discernible difference between them, and from comparing results with local single-sex schools there was no difference there either. Everything centred on 'value added', in that the school should not only get good exam results but should aim to 'add value' so the pupil performed over and above what was expected of them from previous results. So 'highly academic' subjects with a brighter than average cohort had to sometimes strive harder to 'add value.'

Many teaching staff were also examiners with the external boards, and this helped give an insight into exactly what the boards were looking for and therefore the focus and angle for our teaching. Of course, you could not mark scripts from your own centre. Because parental pressure was high and coursework was a major component of the exams, especially GCSE, there was also huge emphasis on encouraging the pupils to produce this work to the highest standard; in some cases it could contribute up to 50% of the final total exam mark. This was marked internally by the teacher and externally moderated by the exam board; the exact final mark would not be known until after the exam results were published. However, most teachers would give a vague indication of the standard, if only to reassure the pupils.

One parent, a professional man respected in the community, objected to the standard given to his offspring and in a letter suggested that it should be re-marked as he had done most of it himself! All this after the pupil had signed an exam board disclaimer saying that, to the best of his/her knowledge, the work was their own! Such 'hovering' parents are now known as 'helicopter parents', i.e. those who want to micro-manage every aspect of their child's life from womb to tomb, interfering in grading and marking and even trying to influence the curriculum. Thankfully, in my experience they were rare, and fee-paying parents were generally very supportive. Inevitably parents could assist in other, more subtle and positive ways, like providing transport for their offspring to access otherwise relatively inaccessible field study sites to collect their coursework data.

The school by now was becoming multi-national in as much as there was a regular intake of Germans and Hong Kong Chinese into the Sixth Form – the latter improving the exam statistics by taking and excelling in GCSE and 'A' Level Chinese with no tuition input from the school.

They all had good spoken English and added much to the culture of the place, not to mention representing the school at various sports and at chess in particular. The latter was particularly strong at the school, with us winning national honours, and there was even an outdoor (summer) walk-on chess board and chess set. Although the bulk of the European pupils came from northern Germany, we believed that the master in charge of European recruitment at the time benefited from large cases of southern German wine which were sometimes conspicuously delivered on site in his name.

Interestingly, in Chinese Mandarin the word for "play" and "go out" are the same. This is okay if the pupils are juniors, but when a Sixth Former tells you that he played with his girlfriend or his wife at the weekend it is time to tell them what the implications might be in English. However, I did say 'go out' at the end of an exam to a Chinese boy and girl, which caused great hilarity – even greater than normally expected at the end of any external exam paper.

Our school, like state schools, later had INSET (In-Service Training) days, also called Baker days after Kenneth Baker, the Secretary of State for Education at the time; these were universally unpopular, as they meant coming back a day earlier from holiday for three terms and the themes up for discussion often seemed peripheral and repetitively cyclical like INSET days. Many headmasters believe that professional development is an essential component of a teacher's growth and prevents more senior colleagues from going stale. On many days a 'course' was introduced and run by a paid guest speaker hired and brought in for the day. On each occasion a note would be passed around amongst most of the staff asking them to guess the speaker's charges, including any hotel bills, for the day; each estimate had to be initialled and accompanied by £1. After consultation with the bursar's secretary who dealt with such matters, the closest 'guestimate' won the kitty.

That said, one INSET topic that all teachers could relate to was 'Bullying: Causes, Consequences and Tackling.' We debated the social and psychological reasons why children might bully – whether it was physical and/or mental abuse. Head of Department B, next to me, was not impressed, especially when it was intimated that we should feel sorry for the bully too. He felt his time would have been better spent at home chopping wood; it was the end of the summer term after all.

The penultimate afternoon session was spent in group discussion of anonymous case studies that had clearly been part of the guest speaker's own research. We were asked how we would deal with them. By this stage B was getting somewhat irate and put his hand up to attract the speaker's attention. He related how he was the Form Tutor of a 14-year-old boy who was a persistent bully of younger boys, forcing them to hand over pocket money or face some kind of physical retribution. When asked how he dealt with it he said "I belted him around the ear and he was no trouble after that." The room erupted in laughter and I believe I heard some muted under-table applause. The lady guest speaker was ashen. Heaven knows how she would have discussed and dealt with cyber-bullying – to be more common in the future. However, some INSET days were more usefully spent, updating first aid skills with mouth-to-mouth on an androgynous dummy.

End-of-day occasional staff meetings were also anticipated with a degree of scepticism. Rather like a class of pupils, the less enthusiastic and more reticent individuals sat as far away as possible from the Headmaster– the first of whom in my experience treated the gatherings as an exercise in eloquent evasion. Hence many issues that should have been investigated by impromptu 'committees' had a habit of resurfacing in a cyclic manner, especially those related to school uniform and its differences of interpretation between staff and pupils. Thirty minutes discussing if there should be any difference in the way boys and girls should knot and wear their ties was interrupted by snoring from the back.

Like our state counterparts, the school had inspections; these were organised and run by the independent sector and so were not OFSTED, but in every other respect resembled them. Back then the school was given advance notice of the inspection team's arrival, so there ensued cleaning, tidying and the putting up of laminated, in some cases previously unused, posters on every available classroom and corridor wall space. Everywhere and anywhere was given at least one coat of paint. First aid boxes mysteriously gained prominence in every laboratory – after dusting. Even the carpet leading to the Head's office was vacuumed to within a millimetre of its backing. Two bonsai trees even appeared at the entrance to the Bursar's office!

Somebody in the Senior Management Team (SMT) said that the school's policy and targets should be "Clear, realistic, achievable and permanent." That was until a member of staff pointed out the acronym for those ideals.

Numerous schemes of work for the junior school began to emerge from the ether, closely paralleling those of the National Curriculum specifications, though the school, unlike its state counterparts, was not legally bound to teach to them. "There have been private schools where there was a syllabus only for the week of the inspection…" (Price, 1960, p.32) Many teachers had previously been given mere departmental guidelines which allowed some flexibility for teachers to give the pupils the benefit of their own personal expertise and interests. Our particular inspector (who looked as if he had last taught when everything was in black and white) was complimentary, but he was particularly keen to take a copy of anything given to the pupils during the lesson observed, e.g. handouts, worksheets, puzzles etc – even contrasting bags of coniferous and deciduous leaf litter. It later emerged that his son was a teacher of the same subject and he wanted to pass on teaching materials to him. As exact numbers of these were done per class size, there were some individuals who were unfortunately left short by his mid-lesson 'theft.' Our visitor seemed to feel he was not a snooper, but more of a missionary.

The French inspector claimed to know all the latest French slang but, when questioned by Mademoiselle D, he revealed that it had been eight years since he was last in France. It was somewhat fortunate that this inspection came immediately after the retirement of one particular French teacher (master). This man was rather eccentric in that he bragged that he could speak with a French dialect to suit any part of the country without being recognised by locals as being a visitor to that area, never mind coming from England. Most staff, and I suspect pupils too, doubted this, as he had a very broad Lancashire accent. However, such was his temper that nobody queried it – especially after it was rumoured that he had once thrown board rubbers around his classroom. I lived two doors down from him for a while and, whilst we exchanged small talk, I was somewhat wary of getting to know him better as I had witnessed one or two of his confrontations with colleagues in the staff room; he seemed a prime candidate for anger management.

Perhaps, somewhat cynically, one department referred to their inspector as a seagull – someone who flies in, makes a lot of noise, craps on everything and then leaves.

One individual Maths teacher was inspected with a Sixth Form set and asked the inspector's advice on a subtle approach to a problem. The said inspector immediately demonstrated his way of tackling it and his exhibition lasted until it was time for him to move on. This particular teacher suggested that inspectors are never so happy as when they are showing off in front of a class, going on to say it was an easy way of earning a living as there was a teacher present to maintain discipline and the class would never see him or her again.

Most inspectors are proud of being vital but seem

It was a choice of watching this or attending a staff meeting...

readier to talk, rather than listen, explaining what they would like to see, rather than noticing what is actually happening – seeing pupils at one moment in time, making judgement of progress difficult.

Fire drills were a necessary diversion from teaching and the time they took to assemble everyone on the playing field meant one less lesson for the pupils, which obviously went down well. One day there was an actual alarm and, embarrassingly, the source of the smoke and therefore the alarm was traced to a teacher having a crafty cigarette between lessons and then hastily discarding the butt in a wastepaper bin, which starting smouldering. The only other full gatherings on the playing fields were for whole school photographs where the pupils were meticulously arranged in tiers by age with all staff at the front and the Headmaster in the middle, seated in an elaborately carved oak chair, somewhat like a Buddha overseeing a meditation retreat. I suspect that second-hand gowns kept in a cupboard somewhere were handed out for the odd non-graduate teachers in the picture.

In the summer terms the teaching staff cricket team played the school First XI in addition to midweek friendlies with local sides, and very sociable it was too. Another member of the teaching clergy regularly turned out for the staff side. In one particular match his son 'guested' for the team, only to be run out by his father, and the square was awash with Anglo-Saxon expletives!

In one particular summer term a supply teacher, A, played for the team. Despite his age and apparent infirmity, he seemed a good acquisition, having said he had played for Leicestershire Seconds in the past. Nobody questioned him about this, but after he had faced a couple of balls it was clear that he no longer had any idea how to bat, if he ever had, and couldn't move very quickly in the field either. He did however revel in the social side after getting through a number of pints in no time the same evening. Unable to get a lift to his distant home, he slept in the staff room, so he was in early for work the next day.

After one particular match I offered him a lift to the railway station to get his last train home. Just before we arrived he shouted "Stop!" He jumped out of the car and briefly apologised; he had seen that one of his favourite watering holes was still open, so he crossed the road and went inside; another night to bed down in the staff room, as the last train had now gone.

After a time we became accustomed to A's stories about himself, though his early disappearance from a parents' evening because there were two mothers in attendance with whom he'd allegedly had affairs was difficult to believe given the age difference – A being much older, especially in appearance, movement and physical coordination.

Parents' evenings were particularly illuminating times, if exhausting. Individual pupils were sometimes unrecognisable from their parents' glowing descriptions of consistent diligence and time spent on homework. Further questioning of both parents and pupil in attendance would often reveal that time spent in their room did not necessarily equate to that spent on school work, with the inevitable backlash on their return home. Many parents here were themselves graduates, both of university and the independent school system, and felt that because it had been a fruitful path for them, their offspring should follow in their footsteps, regardless of their industry, ability and wishes.

The staff also occasionally took on a school leavers' team at football, the First XI being considered too good. Even so, the age, speed and general fitness differential meant the inevitable outcome was a victory for the pupils. But like the school play, it was entertaining for the large crowds that watched and cheered every successful, albeit isolated, staff tackle and pass – sympathy replacing cynicism for those ever-reddening older faces with every minute that passed. Despite this, the staff were very competitive and even managed to fall out amongst themselves over a 'friendly' game of lunch-time croquet on the front lawn; surely a first?

Most of the catering staff were referred to fondly as 'dinner ladies' by the pupils, there being no male equivalent apparently, and these people did an excellent job, especially in meticulously wiping clean the food trays. There were also a number of characters on the kitchen staff too,

"That one taught me English Language that I didn't even learn in the Army."

Daily Express, October 4th, 1984

including one head chef with previous and clearly apparent experience in the army catering, if not the diplomatic, corps. He brought a military bearing to the school dining hall and staff and pupils alike were often ushered in and out like sheep, but without the controlled restraint of a border collie. His newly-introduced dining hall queuing arrangements brought in without prior consultation with either staff or pupils, demanded perverse obedience, and the resultant chaos was for all to see. 'Officers' (Sixth Form) were to be served first at lunch while the 'Privates' (First Years/Year 7s) were fed and watered last. Not surprisingly, given that it had been over two and a half hours since the latter had last eaten anything at all and probably over five hours since breakfast, parents protested about this new arrangement. Sixth Formers after all had access to snacks at any time via a vending machine in their centre. The new queuing system was abandoned within a fortnight.

Similarly, one bursar came from a military officer background and immediately on taking up his post he proceeded to bark orders, rather than make requests, to teaching and maintenance staff alike. In fact, one of the latter was told brusquely that if he was intent on sporting a beard, it should be tidy; otherwise he must be clean shaven. He never mastered the concept that respect in an educational establishment had to be earned, not assumed by rank. He didn't stay long. The previous incumbent, however, was more laid back, and I realised, after visiting him in his office after normal teaching hours, that this may have been due to the bottle of whisky in the top left drawer of his desk, which he slammed smartly shut on my entry.

On the subject of military matters, one teacher, an ex-army officer with a cut-glass accent who was in the TA, ran his school life on military lines. He had a picture of General Buller on his wall and if pupils did or said anything stupid they had to go and apologise to 'the General'. One day he gave one lad a detention for his poor homework and made him go and apologise to 'the General', a standard practice in the lesson. On the lad's return the teacher said, "Well boy, what did the General say?" The pupil replied, "He thought my apology was so good you should let me off the detention." There is no documented response to this.

This member of staff was referred to by the pupils as 'the

Major'. Perhaps somewhat predictably, he was responsible for a variety of activities under the umbrella of 'outdoor education', including 'scout' camps (involving fire-lighting, possibly from dry twig attrition), assault courses, cold/white-water rafting and rock climbing in an abandoned quarry leading to a 'death slide' descent. These pursuits, being extra-curricular, took place at weekends but rarely, if ever, during the summer term. The school intimated that this was necessary to avoid complications and clashes with exams, both internal and external; however, several of the more cynical staff thought 'the Major' took a perverse delight from overseeing what they perceived as otherwise pampered pupils tough it out in the great, chilly outdoors with night marches and suchlike. Either way, despite the burgeoning media career of Ray Mears, the 'Major' cut a solitary figure in the staffroom, often disappearing at lunchtimes to his hut, where he apparently attended to various stored camping equipment and other outdoor-related paraphernalia.

Many voluntary extra-curricular trips, both as part of courses and as holidays, were organised by a range of departments, not only throughout the length of the UK but into mainland Europe, Asia, Africa and the Americas. These yielded many funny stories and anecdotes and I myself managed to get caught up in one of these – literally – when dragging a fairground stall, in the process of being set up, several metres along with a minibus I was driving, leaving an irate man wobbling on a ladder behind. This naturally amused the Sixth Form passengers and the story has been recounted many times since – always with an exaggerated slant, in my opinion.

Whilst the vast majority of trips were successful, both academically and socially, for staff and pupils, it is true that the odd pupil was occasionally 'mislaid', usually left behind in a pub after a careless head count.

Whilst many staff voluntarily gave up their own time for such activities and trips, a newly-appointed Head felt that the staff were obliged to do such things, as it was only to be expected of a fee-paying school. Needless to say, his tenure was characterised by a marked decline in goodwill towards such extra-curricular, out-of-hours commitment.

School minibuses inevitably came in for some rough treatment, frequently returning to base with new indentations and scratches; one member of staff was even reported to the police for crossing double white lines in the road in a school vehicle, collecting some points on his licence and a fine as a result. Perhaps for such reasons the school later leased, rather than owned, such a mode of transport, with 'free' repairs part of the deal.

Of course, staff had to set an example on such trips, especially when unedited articles concerning them later appeared in the school magazine. Mobile phone technology did not help in this respect and videos taken of staff group karaoke sessions late into the evening would soon end up online before any internal censorship opportunity. I'm uncertain if such issues were covered by the later necessary risk assessments and consent forms that had to be completed in detail before such any extra-curricular school trips.

Increasingly, addressing crippling health and safety issues made planning for extra-curricular activities and field trips, e.g. Biology, Geography and Geology, more demanding, as there had been a number of high-profile litigation cases in the national press in other similar schools at this time. This began to make trips to the great outdoors less frequent, despite the opportunities these extra-curricular activities could offer in the way of decision-making, self-discipline and general life skills. This stilted the pupils' opportunities to experience the risks or challenges which life brings us all, leaving them unprepared.

In class too, practical lessons in science and design and technology had to be tailored to comply with new specifications that gave health and safety a much higher profile.

The end of the summer term for the Fifth and Upper Sixth years came immediately before the bulk of their external exams; it was their last day of teaching at school and something to celebrate. Eccentricities of uniform on the day, various posters and other items placed about the campus overnight were originally par for the course.

Once there was even a boat in the quad, with its designer/occupant resplendent in a striped 1920s bathing costume and sunglasses, all embedded in about two tonnes of sand under a beach parasol. Once a small flock of sheep was driven by a farmer's son, with the aid of a collie, across the playing fields, and a teacher's moped was taped fast to the roof of the Sixth Form building. These annual 'incidents' were an inconvenience to say the least, especially to the maintenance staff who had to clear up the aftermath. Early attempts to limit them concentrated on diversionary tactics such as providing a leavers' barbecue and a bouncy castle on the day. This however went awry when a Fifth Former bounced off the inflatable onto the playing field, dislocating a shoulder in the process. Being in part a boarding establishment, there was always a day duty nurse on campus, normally ready to dispense paracetamol for any (minor) ailment, but on this occasion she quickly sent the pupil to hospital.

This kind of leavers' day, which left the site at best messy, as opposed to vandalised, was later minimised by continuous patrols across the school campus through the previous night. Previous final assembly pleas from successive earlier heads imploring restraint on leavers' day had failed. Some of the teaching staff wallowed in the clear discomfort faced by the senior management team in dealing with this issue, feeling that it was high time pupil discipline was faced head on, rather than delegated to the more poorly-paid minions.

Practical jokes were commonplace in the school, especially staff on staff. However, when a member of the teaching staff repeatedly received letters in his pigeon hole from Alcoholics Anonymous about how they could help him, it began to irritate the recipient after a time; quite who set this up is still unknown, though there was a short list of about twelve, who would have constituted a diverse academic identity parade.

Over time the teaching staff had to become more familiar with IT and the use of interactive whiteboards which replaced blackboards; some did so on a need-to-know basis, whilst others undertook voluntary courses at school. However, the network manager, who would be called to deal with the slightest problem with computing, always worked on the assumption that it was a user error or misunderstanding rather than a technological fault; he was usually correct in that.

Like most schools of its type, by the 1990s ours had a Director of Studies (D of S) whose responsibility was to oversee the curriculum and those delivering it. This was effectively the responsibility of putting into practice another man's policy. The more cynical amongst the teaching staff felt that the creation of the post was more a response to the Head's need for a henchman, there to finger any member of staff perceived to be not up to scratch or pulling his/her weight with a particular class or area of the syllabus

"DON'T WORRY BOYS, I HAVE YOUR CONSENT FORMS."

or specifications. Some perceived this as doing the Head's dirty work; an abdication of responsibility by him.

Needless to say, this brought the D of S into conflict with certain members of staff who felt their professionalism and competence were being brought into question. This did manifest itself in the form of a physical attack in one case and numerous threats of such in a few others. However, for the best part, the teaching staff had a family feel about it; some were former pupils themselves, and indeed had been taught by individuals who were still there. Also, there were a few husband and wife 'teams' on the staff – in some cases in the same department – not to mention a number of staff offspring on the pupil roll. Social harmony became more

"All these millions they're spending on education make these pipe racks come out pretty dear Christmas presents."

obvious with time and convivial end-of-term Christmas 'dos' were attended by the vast majority of the teaching staff and their partners.

Pupil recollections are also very funny and the following stand out: an English teacher getting his class to do a conga outside when a certain pupil got a question right for the first time; a pupil catching a 3am bus for a history trip when he hadn't done the subject for two years; a pupil woken up by a Russian prostitute in a Moscow hotel on a school trip; a pupil on a camping trip eating sheep's droppings, having been told by another that they were chocolate muffins.

Excellent exam results suggested that the vast majority of the teaching staff spouted words of wisdom for much of the time, though verbatim quotes in the yearly school magazine might suggest otherwise. For example, "I was caned at school – and I loved it." And/or: "I can't wear shorts because my legs have been waxed."

"This only **seems** dangerous." (Chemistry teacher)

"I've developed a nut fetish recently."

"ICT – what's ICT?"

"If you get one of these questions in the exam, you can spank me."

"Writing a bad introduction is like passing wind on a first date."

"My wife's commands go out as an order of the Führer."

Or, better still, from the Maths department: "You must use the x-axis – or you could use the other one."

"I learnt how to get pictures off the internet, especially from Amsterdam."

"This tea is different – it's made of leaves."

"The thing with biology is that it's all about sex or poo."

"Now we know that women are the master race."

"If you're impotent, the matter won't arise."

Pupils, too, offer similar, perhaps unintentional, witticisms; for example (a Sixth Former after a French exchange visit): "Their music leaves a lot to be desired." Other Sixth Form quotes include: "Neil and Louis Armstrong – were they brothers?" "The goal of all Buddhists is to reach Nevada." "How many counters do you have to connect to win in Connect 4?" "The Huns – they were Japanese, weren't they?" and finally "Is cannibalism illegal?"

These 'words of wisdom' were frequently remembered verbatim, often with some fondness, by both past and present pupils when they met up with the present staff.

The pupils also ran an 'Agony Aunt' (AA) column in the annual school magazine, and staff turned to that page first. Examples of (tongue in cheek) questions and advice are summarized below:

"Dear AA, I am taking Maths and Physics 'A' Level and want to study engineering. Am I turning into a boring vegetable?"

Auntie: "Have you considered teaching?"

"Dear AA, In an effort to upgrade my image, I painted my car green and put on some gold hub caps. This failed to have the desired effect. I was wondering if you think that leopard skin seat covers and a pair of large furry dice would help?"

Auntie: "You sound like a person of excellent taste.

Perhaps you could advise me on a colour scheme for my new kitchen? I was thinking of lime green pebble dash walls with a mauve Artex ceiling and gold-sprayed kitchen units and a waterfall effect in the corner. Yes, I know it's copied from the plans for the new theatre."

"Dear AA, I have recently found out that platform shoes and 22-inch flares are unfashionable after wearing them for years."

Auntie: "Why don't you become a Maths teacher? The addition of a bright red shirt with big lapels would guarantee you instant success."

As the US author and teacher Robert Wilder said when asked by the speaker at the end of the American equivalent of an INSET day if there was anything else teachers needed, his reply said "Yes, we all need someone to teach us to dress!" (Wilder, 2007, p.283)

Over time the use of interactive whiteboards became widespread, with one in each classroom, together with attendant screen and PC. Now anything on the internet could be used as a teaching aid, along with the teacher's own prepared lesson work, including personal Power Point presentations with photos, movie clip links and DVDs. This made learning more interesting and education fun, both for the pupils and some of the staff; a few of the more senior teachers felt that the whiteboards were better suited to business, rather than an educational resource. But the school was a business.

Perhaps, less fondly, with the more common use of increasingly sophisticated technology, there has been an exponential rise in the use of mobile phones for pupils and this has led to a similar rise in the tendency to talk and especially write in 'textspeak.' The handwritten strange or funny 'words' that appear are not found in The Oxford English Dictionary and often comprise letters and numbers somewhat like an unfinished password.

The largest examination boards were (and still are) making general complaints about this to schools and returned, re-marked papers certainly seem to support this – even in my time. Common usage of 'm8' for mate, 'u' for you and '2' for to or too were initially comical, but of

Always label your axes

course they undermine the fabric and use of the English language. Nobody, to the best of my knowledge, ever used 'copul8.' It wasn't as if these modernisms weren't being corrected at my school – pupils are writing and reading far more texts than essays or books in day-to-day life; it was force of habit, and these are fast becoming standard abbreviations in communication for some.

In addition to texting variations on the language, teachers detected new phrases (often patronising, sexist and politically incorrect) introduced into pupils' language, such as the following overheard directly in school or read from mobile phones:

'Salad dodger' - a degrading term for an overweight person.

'Swamp donkey' – a deeply unattractive person.

'Percussive maintenance' – the fine art of whacking the hell out of an electronic device to get it to work.

'Sprung' (adjective) – deeply in love or obsessed.

'Tramp stamp' – more than one tattoo on a female. Surely very sexist and of course mainly heard from boys.

Chapter 5

Reflection

Whilst teaching is a serious and responsible career, motivating young enquiring minds and stimulating curiosity, it frequently has a funny side from the perspective of the pupils, and especially one's colleagues. The latter, whose effectiveness is often proportional to their eccentricity, made me laugh regularly – whether intentionally or not. I am indebted to them for that. Eccentricity, natural or not, arouses interest and stimulates curiosity. Anything odd or strange may be accompanied by off-beat humour, and all of this makes the process of education easier for all parties involved.

Having worked in most types of secondary school (modern, comprehensive and independent), maybe I've been lucky, but most teenagers have and appreciate a sense of humour and I certainly do not believe, as one author comically put it, that "They should be shot into space until they reach their mid-20s." (Quantick, 2004, p.112)

Teaching is a calling, and with it comes a great responsibility to present pupils with the facts and not imbue them with your own values and attitudes; let them make up their own minds. It is during this apparently serious progression that laughter can help with the process, especially when it's spontaneous.

If most of the comic sources in this piece of work originate from staff, it is because of the perception, even amongst colleagues, that teachers should always be strait-laced and sober in every sense of the word; in short, living, walking examples of responsible moderation. When they appear anything less and veer towards eccentricity they can become very funny – a fact enjoyed by pupils and colleagues alike.

'Trust me. If they do ban mobile phones in schools, you will gradually learn to speak without one.'

Bibliography, References and Sources

Giles/Express Newspapers/Express Syndication.

Mac/Mail Newspapers/Mail Syndication

Hal Urban. "Lesson #1: Good teachers share one special quality." Chapter One in *Lessons from the Classroom: 20 Things Good Teachers Do*, Saline, MI: Great Lesson Press, 2008, 1-10.

Owen M (2014) *Who'd be a teacher?* Create Space Independent Publishing Platform

Phinn, G (2004) *The School Inspector Calls*, London, Penguin

Price RGG (1960) *How to Become Headmaster*, London, Anthony Blond

Quantick, D (2004) *Grumpy Old Men*, London, Harper Collins

Sharpe, T (2002) *Vintage Stuff* London Arrow

Wilder R (2007) *Tales from the Teacher's Lounge*, New York, Random House

Ziv, A (1979) *L'humour en education: approche psychologique*, Paris Social Françaises

The Times (08/09/1989)

https://archive.cartoons.ac.uk/GetMultimedia.ashx?db=Catalog&type=default&fname=28512.jpg

https://archive.cartoons.ac.uk/GetMultimedia.ashx?db=Catalog&type=default&fname=GAA091127.jpg

https://archive.cartoons.ac.uk/GetMultimedia.ashx?db=Catalog&type=default&fname=54198.jpg

https://archive.cartoons.ac.uk/GetMultimedia.ashx?db=Catalog&type=default&fname=96511.jpg

http://www.gilescartoons.co.uk

www.cartoonstock.com

http://www.john-leech-archive.org.uk/1853/knowledge-is-power.htm

http://www.motivationalplus.com/Cartoonsforteachers.html

https://uk.pinterest.com/pin/

http://www.thefreedictionary.com/funny

Printed in Poland
by Amazon Fulfillment
Poland Sp. z o.o., Wrocław